THE ROMA SERIES

LEONARD VON MATT

RENAISSANCE

ART IN ROME

COMMENTARY BY VALERIO MARIANI

UNIVERSE BOOKS NEW YORK

First American Edition
published in the United States of America in 1961 by
UNIVERSE BOOKS, Inc.
381 Park Avenue South
New York 16, New York
Library of Congress Catalog Card Number 61-14583

Printed in Switzerland

"Iacent domus, labant moenia, templa ruunt, sacra pereunt."
(The houses are in ruins, the walls are abandoned, the temples are crumbling away, the sanctuaries are falling to dust.)

These agonized words were uttered by Petrarch as he contemplated the ruin and the desolation of Rome in his day. They indicate more graphically than any other eyewitness account the lamentable state into which the city had fallen during the exile of the Popes in Avignon.

At the very time when the larger Italian cities were entering upon a period of astonishing prosperity and when Florence above all was on the verge of initiating the Renaissance, Rome was torn by bitter strife among contending families and brawling factions. Moreover, it had been depopulated except for a few districts in the lower part of the city between the Campo Marzio, the Velabro and the Tiber. The population eked out a precarious existence in the shadow of the gigantic ruins of Imperial Rome between the strongholds of the noble families and the basilicas, themselves partly in ruins.

Upon the return of the Popes to the capital of Christendom any immediate renewal of artistic activity was hardly thinkable; it was difficult enough merely to cope with the most urgent needs of practical, everday life. It was only under Martin V (1417–1431) that building was resumed in Rome, and this was at first restricted, to be sure, to the reconstruction and the renovation, above all, of the Vatican, the Lateran and the major churches. Under Eugene IV, who was banished from Rome for nine years, and under Nicholas V (1447–55), the city gradually began to alter its visage, receiving inspiration from Florence, from which city the Popes invited an ever increasing number of celebrated artists.

Nicholas V possessed a vision that was worthy of Rome: he was the first to conceive of an organic plan for the city, and Leon Battista Alberti set about its realization with all the enthusiasm of a humanist and the mastery of an inspired architect.

Also under Pius II, the humanist Enea Silvio Piccolomini, but especially under the Venetian Paul II, much was done to restore the city to its former splendor; the first Renaissance palaces were erected, streets and squares were paved, bridges restored, and long forgotten water conduits which had so abundantly supplied the city in imperial times were reopened.

However, it was only under Sixtus IV (1471–1484) that Rome assumed a radically new appearance, marked not only by individual buildings and restorations but by the entire complex of structures that the great Pope (justly known as "restaurator urbis") had erected, along modern lines and for the benefit of all the citizens. His works include the Santo Spirito Hospital, the Ponte Sisto, groups of palaces and houses conceived according to an uniform plan, churches in the new Renaissance style, bold constructions like the Sistine Chapel.

The Rome of the 15th century is decidedly the Rome of Sixtus IV, and it was the example of this indefatigable and persevering Pope that inspired the great pontiffs of the 16th century, from Julius II and Leo X to Paul III and Sixtus V.

It is therefore not surprising if Rome, which during the Middle Ages and above all in the 13th century had enjoyed periods of artistic splendor that seemed to herald the advent of the Renaissance, was slow

to reacquire a monumental aspect. Only at the end of the 15th century did it again become a magnet for leading artists and the great center of art and culture in general.
It was, in fact, political and religious circumstances that broke the rhythm of steady development and delayed by nearly a century the full realization of the Renaissance spirit.
If, as a consequence, Rome did not benefit from the presence of the great artists of the early 15th century, especially architects and sculptors (from Ghiberti to Brunelleschi, from Donatello to Leon Battista Alberti, who left here only a few traces of their work), the city of the Popes nevertheless had gathered within its walls those active at the end of the century as well as all the great masters of the 16th century. Under Sixtus IV there were Antonio and Piero del Pollaiolo and the painters of the Sistine Chapel: Sandro Botticelli, Perugino, Luca Signorelli, Pinturicchio, then Bramante, Raphael, Michelangelo, Sansovino, Benvenuto Cellini, Sebastiano del Piombo, Titian and a throng of artists and craftsmen.
The journey to Rome, which from the end of the medieval period had been eagerly undertaken by artists, poets, men of culture and of the Church, becomes in the Renaissance the ultimate ambition of every artist. The new style had in Florence, its birthplace, rediscovered the harmony and the beauty of Antiquity, but in Rome it came into direct contact with the architectural monumentality of the imperial age, the rich variety of classical sculpture and the atmosphere created by these walls and arches that still conveyed the splendor of the imperial epoch.
The Renaissance artists acquired in Rome a new sense of grandeur, their conception of proportions was amplified, their horizons were extended and their sculptural and pictorial compositions were intensified. Bramante's idea for the new St. Peter's, Michelangelo's conceptions for the tomb of Julius II and the ceiling of the Sistine Chapel and the "Scuola d'Atene" of Raphael, are, to be sure, the expression of the individual genius of these artists; their imagination could unfold, however, in the specific form in which it did unfold, nowhere but in Rome. Rome was a profound inspiration for the Renaissance artists not only in that it served to embody their highest ideals but also in that it was a creative environment where, as the poet expresses it, "everything is great and exalted."
The fact – as reported by Vasari – that Brunelleschi and Donatello undertook in secret a journey to Rome immediately after the prize competition for the new door of the Baptistery in Florence, is the clearest evidence of the already lively aspiration to come into direct contact with the Holy City and its immense wealth of architecture and sculpture, some of it still to be unearthed. It also testifies to the spirit of discovery animating the artists of this epoch. Rome could not be for these two Tuscans, any more than for Ghiberti, a permanent place of work, but the city afforded them, as it did so many later artists, an immediate and jealously cherished experience of Antiquity. The Roman sojourn of Leon Battista Alberti had a more concrete effect; Alberti came here when Masolino had already painted in San Clemente, when Fra Angelico was working in the Vatican and Piero della Francesca too was decorating the Papal palaces.
1 The first palace erected in Rome in the monumental spirit, the Palazzo Venezia, can – though unfinished – be regarded as striking evidence of the presence in Rome of Leon Battista Alberti, not only for its magnificence, its similarity to the buildings of Rossellino in Pienza (executed by Rossellino from designs by Leon Battista Alberti) but also for the endeavor here to observe geometrical proportions. The Palace, which rose as an extension of the Palazzo Barbo, a property of the future Paul II, was to have had three

additional square towers at the corners and a central courtyard, and was to include within its walls the ancient basilica of San Marco (this part of the plan being executed). The "cruciate" windows so common in Rome are here developed in a style that is deliberately severe, while the marvellous courtyard, only half completed, is one of the first and best examples of Renaissance architecture in the papal city. Various other Roman palaces were constructed with this as a model in the second half of the 15th century. They still convey some idea of the bare austerity of the Middle Ages.

A decisive step in the application of the Renaissance style was the construction of the Palace of the Cancelleria, sponsored by the rich nephew of Sixtus IV, Raffaele Riario. Here too the architect (who remains unknown) took his inspiration from the palaces of Florence and Urbino. The ancient church of SS. Lorenzo and Damaso was incorporated in the new plan to form a huge architectural complex, within which the goldsmiths' shops in the Via del Pellegrino and even the asymmetrical course of the old street were preserved.

The Palace of the Cancelleria, which was imitated in various other Roman buildings (like the Palazzo Giraud Torlonia in the Via della Conciliazione) brings us to the major architect of the period, Donato Bramante. He no sooner arrives in Rome than he begins to transform the visage of the still architecturally inchoate city.

Having left Milan to come to Rome, Bramante conceives gigantic reorganization plans and is furthered in his endeavors by the great Pope Julius II.

We have now reached the point when Rome entered upon her most glorious period. The city was becoming the major center of attraction for men of learning and artists from all over Europe. Bramante succeeded finally in realizing a conception that was to be taken up later by so many artists, that is, "vedere in grande" (to see things on a vast scale).

The Tempietto of San Pietro in Montorio is a building that concretely embodies the classical architectural ideal of the Renaissance (the church has a central plan); it stands in Rome as a perfect example of the resurgence of classical harmony: the type of architecture which the Renaissance had dreamed of as its ideal and which the painters had employed in the backgrounds of their pictures has here finally become a reality and was subsequently to serve as a model and standard.

Bramante pushed forward his architectural program with the cloister of Santa Maria della Pace (1504) and the grandiose and lucidly conceived courtyard of the Cancelleria; it comprises in addition the tracing out of the "Via Giulia" and the planning of the foundations of the Tribunale, but, above all else, the monumental projects in the Vatican and St. Peter's: the Belvedere, with its gigantic niche commanding a panorama of the city and the numerous buildings so brilliantly integrated with the old medieval structures and, finally, his plan for the reconstruction of the basilica in the shape of a centrally planned church surmounted by an immense dome.

Bramante's creative will was seconded by the wishes of Julius II: having torn down the apse (he was known to the populace as "Maestro Ruinante," the "Master of Destruction") and having erected the mighty columns which–inspired by the Pantheon–were to support the dome, he died without seeing his dream realized. However, his presence in Rome was decisive and all the architects who worked here after him were, though in various ways, under the sway of his mastery.

2

3

5

With Bramante new horizons were disclosed to Roman architecture: the palaces of the noble families were now harmoniously integrated with their surroundings: the streets and squares became scenic vantage points and at the same time the oldest churches had their façades and porticoes transformed and their interiors furnished with gilt and carved coffered ceilings, and the chapels of the nobility received splendid monuments.

Nevertheless, this flourishing period of the arts and of Roman life in general was abruptly and tragically terminated by the Sack of Rome in 1527. The city was already famous for its wealth of monuments: the noble families vied with one another in embellishing their palaces; there were erected charming villas in the green environs of the city like the Villa Madama, designed by Raphael and carried out by Giulio Romano; the "Farnesina," belonging to the great banker Agostino Chigi, was built by Baldassare Peruzzi and was decorated by the major artists of the time, Peruzzi himself, Sebastiano del Piombo, Sodoma and Raphael with his already famous school.

36–39

One must turn to the pages of the "Vita," the autobiography of Benvenuto Cellini, dealing with the Sack of Rome and the siege of the Castel Sant'Angelo to form some idea of the tragedy that befell the city almost like a dire admonition with the entrance of the Lanzichenecchi, the looting of the major princely palaces and the precipitate exodus of the artists and men of letters in quest of other patrons in quieter cities.

Nevertheless, the proof that the progress of Rome in the 16th century was the outpouring of a spontaneous vital creativity and that henceforth the city would be a focus of artistic activity unique in the world is to be found in the rapid recovery of the Urbs after 1527. Many of the artists who had left Rome as a city of ruins returned. Even more magnificent buildings were erected than in the early part of the century. On the papal way where there already stood the Palaces of the Cancelleria, Vidoni-Caffarelli (designed by Raphael) and the Palazzo della Valle, Baldassarre Peruzzi created the Palazzo Massimo alle Colonne in the solemn 16th century style, the sole example of a curving façade. Somewhat later Antonio da Sangallo built the immense Palazzo Farnese, upon which Michelangelo was to leave his mark. During this period, almost as testimony to the new Roman monumentality, there rose the Campidoglio, the creation of Michelangelo, as an ideal focus for the holy city. Here in the center of this harmonious square is where the bronze statue of Marcus Aurelius was put up, which had formerly stood in St. John Lateran. Also the renovation of the basilica of St. Peter's, on which Raphael, Peruzzi and Antonio da Sangallo had worked after Bramante, was pushed forward decisively by the naming of Michelangelo as architect of all the buildings in the Vatican. Already an old man, but indomitable and tenacious in his approach to gigantic projects, Michelangelo took in hand the immense task and nearly completed it with the construction of the enormous foundation, of the apses closely related by the order of the pillars and of the tambour with its double columns upon which was to rise the dome, following his design. At the time of his death on February 18, 1564, he could already contemplate the enormous mass of the basilica, which lacked only the vaulting. His dream, which was the dream as well of so many Popes and of all Christendom, became a reality before the close of the 16th century under Sixtus V; and the dome of St. Peter's, rearing up on the Roman skyline, became the symbol of an entire epoch.

4

6

7

46–48

The ever more grandiose architectural setting of Renaissance Rome gave a new vital impulse as well to the arts of sculpture and painting. The great bronze door that Filarete executed for the Vatican basilica, as intricately magnificent as a work of the goldsmith's art and rich in Renaissance motifs, marks the transformation that had overtaken all artistic aspirations. Even more promising was the flourishing of plastic art in the marble sculptures of Mino da Fiesole, Mino del Reame, Giovanni Dalmata, Andrea Bregno.

The tomb of Paul II for the old St. Peter's is a consummate example of Tuscan art in Rome, a work of Mino da Fiesole and of his colleagues, who decorated the chapels of the churches with altars and masterful 14–16 sculptures, after having already created those masterpieces: the great transept and the choir of the Sistine Chapel.

In the time of Sixtus IV the Tuscan and Lombard artists had already flocked in considerable numbers to Rome: everywhere we come across their splendid and consummately executed marble decorations, drawing directly on motifs to be found in classical sculpture. However, the dominant artist of this group was Pollaiolo, who with his brother Piero left two major works: the tombs of Sixtus IV and of Innocent VIII, 20–21 the former completed in 1493, the latter in 1498. The magnificent tomb of Sixtus IV (now in the Vatican crypt) executed according to a radically new conception represents the Pope reclining on an rich catafalque, just as though his body were still exposed to the veneration of the faithful. This tomb, modeled in bronze with extraordinary vivacity and refinement, is the supreme example of 15th century sculpture in Rome; around the figure of the Pope the artist – doubtless advised by humanists and prelates – has grouped the Virtues and, around the base, the Sciences including, along with Theology, Philosophy, 22–25 Logic, Rhetoric and Grammar, as well as Astronomy, Music, Geometry and Perspective. The latter is a new science introduced by the Renaissance on an equal footing with the others as an element of modern culture.

The tomb of Innocent VIII (re-erected in St. Peter's) was, on the other hand, conceived as a mural tomb, with the figure of the Pontiff appearing twice: enthroned in awful majesty and in the holy simplicity of death.

At the beginning of the 16th century Andrea and Jacopo Sansovino iniatated a new development in Renaissance mortuary art in Rome. The former carved for the choir of Santa Maria del Popolo the tomb of Cardinal Ascanio Sforza (1505) and that of Girolamo Basso della Rovere (1507). They reproduced the likeness of the deceased more monumentally than before, their work resembling in this respect the 26–27 Etruscan urns. The figures are no longer represented as frozen in the immobility of death but immersed, as it were, in profound thought with head raised and supported by an arm.

Jacopo Sansovino, before emigrating to Venice during the Sack of Rome, had already furnished proof of his classicism in various churches and, above all, with the magnificent group of the "Vergine del Parto" in the church of Sant'Agostino, created in 1521 under the obvious influence of both classical art and of Michelangelo.

Michelangelo towered above all the other sculptors in Rome in the 16th century. His renowned "Pietà," 40 created at the order of Cardinal Villier de la Groslaye for the oratorium of Santa Petronilla (next to the Vatican basilica) and subsequently erected in the first chapel of the right aisle of the new St. Peter's upon its completion, makes him the greatest sculptor of his time.

This Pietà, which inaugurates the 16th century, takes up the motif of Christ in death lying in the arms of

His Mother and instills it with the most intense dramatic expressiveness: the sensibility of the artist is expressed in the extraordinarily incisive clarity of the sculptural composition. The light falls on the frail body of Chirst while dense shadows are formed by the folds of the Virgin's robes, producing what could be regarded as a heroic figure of a Niobe spiritualized by the intensity of Christian inwardness. Justly proud of his masterpiecce, Michelangelo, by way of exception, signed this work on the band passing across the breast of the Madonna. And centuries of constant and fervid admirers of this celebrated group have justified the artist.

In Rome Michelangelo designed for Julius II the gigantic papal mausoleum to be erected beneath the dome of St. Peter's as planned by Bramante. The first design comprised a double quadrangular base with statues of prophets and sibyls and surrounded by slaves in chains symbolizing the arts that were no longer free after the death of the great Pontiff. Of the forty-four statues which the artist had planned there were completed only those of the slaves, now in the Louvre and in the Academy of Florence and the Moses in San Pietro in Vincoli. The latter famous sculpture, representing suppressed anger immediately before its outburst, became a model for those artists who were reacting against the ornamental grace of the 15th century.

42–44

41

Another profoundly moving work by Michelangelo is the Christ triumphant holding the Cross, executed at the order of Metello Vari between 1514 and 1521 for the church of Santa Maria sopra Minerva, where it still stands today to the left of the high altar beneath which rests the body of St. Catherine of Siena.

Sculpture in the 16th century in Rome developed in the main under the influence of Michelangelo, though having some of its severity modified at times by contact with reality; this can be seen in the elegant bronze figures of the "tortoise fountain" in the Piazza Mattei, designed under Sixtus V by Giacomo della Porta (1585). The slender figures of the youths pushing the tortoises on the edge of the upper basin are the exquisite creations of Taddeo Landini; they remind one of the statue of Jonah created by Lorenzetto following a design of Raphael and now standing in the Chigi Chapel of Santa Maria del Popolo.

30

The tomb of Paul III Farnese in St. Peter's can be considered the rich conclusion of 16th century sculpture in Rome. It is the work of Guglielmo della Porta and was for a time standing free in the Tribuna of the Vatican basilica, then set up as part of a symmetrical group with the tomb of Urban VIII, by Bernini. Guglielmo della Porta, perhaps following up an idea of Michelangelo, shows the Pope enthroned, flanked by four marble statues: Justice and Prudence (still to be seen at the tomb) as well as Bounty and Charity (now in the Palazzo Farnese). The Papal Tomb possesses a monumental grandeur and aristocratic magnificence that fully express the spirit of Rome in the 16th century.

The new Renaissance painters began to arrive in Rome in the opening decades of the 15th century. Masolino gave contemporary painters and those who came after him one of the clearest examples of the Florentine style of painting in his frescoes in the Chapel of St. Catherine of Alexandria in San Clemente.

His narrative gift combined with the gentle sweetness of his figures and the delicacy of his colors brings us to the dawn of the 15th century. Above all, his great altar painting, the "Crucifixion," announces the new spirit with its delicate chromatic transitions studied from nature.

Eugene IV had admired Fra Angelico in Florence and subsequently invited him to Rome, where he arrived in 1445. He was preceded by the fame he had already won for himself with the frescoes in the Cloister of San Marco. The painter-friar was the guest of his fellow monks in the Cloister of the Minerva and set to work at once in the Vatican painting a chapel (since destroyed) that was completed at the death of the Pope in 1447. However, he has left the second wonderful "Cappella Nicolina," executed at the order of Nicholas V in the old 13th century tower of the Vatican. 32

On February 18, 1455, Fra Angelico died and was buried in Santa Maria della Minerva; his monument represents him sleeping in the immobility of death.

Piero della Francesca sojourned only a short while in Rome. Nevertheless, he left his mark on the painters of the time: Antoniazzo Romano and Lorenzo da Viterbo, while there remain of the work of Melozzo da Forli, an impressively solemm artist, the creator of original compositions making use of persepective, the fragments of what was certainly the most important decorative painting of those years in Rome: the apse of the church of Santi Apostoli. The trumpeting angels surrounding Christ in glory are in the Vatican Gallery, and the central part of the fresco showing Christ in the midst of seraphim is in the Quirinale Palace.

At that time the Vatican Library was being renovated, and Platina (the celebrated author of the "Vita Pontificum") had himself portrayed by Melozzo kneeling before Sixtus IV in the library bathed in light, in the presence of dignitaries; the fresco is one of the treasures of the Vatican Gallery and is eloquent testimony to the influence of Humanism at the end of the 15th century.

When the Sistine Chapel was completed, which, along with the Ponte Sisto and the Santo Spirito Hospital, testifies to the astounding architectural vision of Sixtus IV, the greatest artists then living in Florence were invited to decorate the walls of the new Chapel with frescoes worthy of the place. There came to Rome Sandro Botticelli, Ghirlandaio, Cosimo Rosselli, Luca Signorelli, Perugino, Pinturicchio, with numerous assistants. Botticelli was placed in charge of the whole undertaking and commissioned to execute most of the frescoes; he is responsible for the painted architectural subdivisions of the walls, the three paintings: "Sacrifice of the Leper," "Legends of Moses" and "Punishment of the Rebellious Priests" as well as some of the figures of Popes in the niches, which invest the whole with a solemn dignity. In the total pictorial complex there can be seen side by side consummate works from two schools of painting, the Florentine and the Umbrian.

Sandro Botticelli here developed his elegant and sensitive narrative style creating a masterpiece in the "Legends of Moses." Perugino with his famous "Delivery of the Keys" opened the wall, as it were, to the illusion of space and drew portraits that fairly breathe with life and concentrated energy. The great project was completed between 1481 and 1483.

Soon thereafter Pinturicchio created in the apartment of Alexander VI Borgia a further example of the graceful decorative style of the 15th century. This artist also enjoyed an enormous success with his many frescoes in the churches of Santa Maria del Popolo and Santa Maria in Aracoeli.

However, with the accession of Julius II, all this seemed too sweet and cloying; the same painters who were working in the new papal apartment in the Vatican, Sodoma, Baldassare Peruzzi and Bramantino, could no longer meet all the demands for majestic grandeur on the part of the Pope and his court. At this moment Raphael appeared in Rome, at the instigation of Bramante, to work in the Vatican, and Michel-

45 angelo incarcerated himself in the Sistine Chapel, where, stretched out on an enormous scaffold, he painted the great ceiling, between 1508 and 1512. This work astounded his contemporaries and represented a new departure in art.

These were the decisive years for Italian painting; it attained in Rome a grandeur never before seen and began to radiate its influence throughout the world.

Raphael and Michelangelo were painting here at the same time, the former in the "Stanze," the latter in the Sistine Chapel. Raphael began his work in the "Stanza della Segnatura," whose vibrant compositions opened up new horizons for art. In the "Disputà del Sacramento" there are still to be detected reverberations of the 15th century manner; in the "Scuola d'Atene," the major masterpiece of the Renaissance, reflecting all the ideals and aspirations of the artists and men of learning of the time, he reveals himself already as a painter of astonishing mangnificence; in the "Messa di Bolsena," and in the "Freeing of St. Peter," finally, he fuses consummately the color effects of the Venetians and the chiaroscuro of Michelangelo.

Michelangelo, in the meantime, realized in the Sistine a grandiose complex of painted architecture into which were inserted the story of Creation, prophets and sibyls, exalted and mighty figures whose force of expression and heroism of spirit the 15th century had not even dreamed of. The fusion of design, chiaroscuro, color instills a new feeling into the human form, the highest ideal of the Renaissance, given its mightiest expression by the plastic power of Michelangelo. Along the walls beneath the 15th century frescoes there were hung the tapestries woven in Brussels from designs by Raphael; one can well imagine the extraordinary nobility and richness of the Sistine Chapel on solemn occasions after Michelangelo had finished the ceiling and the tapestries were in place. From the airily conceived choir of Mino da Fiesole resounded the voices of the renowned "Cappella," priests and high dignitaries surrounded the Pope in their sumptuously colored vestments, while through the clouds of incense the prophets and sibyls of Michelangelo looked down in meditation or inspired with the divine afflatus, and God the Father with awful majesty created the world.

Much later–from 1534 to 1541–Michelangelo painted, at the order of Paul III, behind the altar of the Sistine Chapel, the "Last Judgment," a profoundly tragic testimony to the spiritual upheaval of the 16th century. Michelangelo, who was already commissioned by Clement VII to paint the enormous wall was constrained to obey the new Pope and cover the vast area of nearly 200 square meters with the dramatic composition inspired by the "Dies Irae" with vivid allusions to the world of Dante. Michelangelo conjured up in the depths of his imagination the theme of the last act of Divine Justice: humanity resurrected and summoned before Christ ("Rex tremendae Majestatis") struggles in an atmosphere of overwhelming gloom and terror, in which the separation between Good and Evil takes the form of a gigantic battle. The painter reveals those summoned to Judgment in their original nakedness, bereft of all signs of the luxury or the penury attending them during their mundane existences.

The work gave rise to passionate controversy but has remained through the centuries a profound testimony to the tragic crisis in the spirit of that age, which was called the Golden Age but which in its very exaltation of life perhaps overstepped the bounds of perfect harmony and disrupted the balance among ideals and aspirations which had been at the basis of the Renaissance conception of man.

CAPTIONS TO THE ILLUSTRATIONS

Table 1

Palazzo Venezia. Cardinal Pietro Barbo began the construction of this severe palace in 1452. The first structure consisted of the massive medieval tower and a square building. After his election as Pope (Paul II) in 1464 he had the palace enlarged; his plan envisaged four towers at the corners, and perhaps originated with Leon Battista Alberti. The work was completed after the death of the Pope, but not in accordance with the extensive plan appearing on the medallion of Paul II.

Table 2

Palazzo Venezia. Courtyard. The courtyard has two rows of arcades and produces an effect of harmony and solemnity. It was only half completed, but it reveals, nevertheless, the genius of a great architect of the middle years of the 15th century, probably Leon Battista Alberti.

Table 3

Palazzo della Cancelleria. Courtyard. The Palazzo della Cancelleria, built by the nephew of Sixtus IV, Cardinal Raffaele Riario, is the most sumptuous and vast of the century. It was completed at the end of the 15th century; the courtyard, dating from 1511, is the work of Bramante, and it recalls in the harmony of its architectural disposition the Ducal Palace of Urbino.

Table 4

Palazzo Massimo alle Colonne. Interior of the entrance portico. An original and severe work of the architect and painter Baldassare Peruzzi, who completed it in 1535. A peculiarity of the Palazzo Massimo is its curving façade following the old "Via Papale" (now Corso Vittorio Emanuele), along which passed processions and pilgrimages on the way to St. Peter's.

Table 5

San Pietro in Montorio. Tempietto by Bramante. A masterpiece of the great architect, constructed shortly after his arrival in Rome in 1502. It exemplifies most clearly the architectural ideals of the Renaissance. Taking his inspiration from classical designs (including the so-called "Temple of Vesta") and also from Piero della Francesca, Laurana and Francesco di Giorgio Martini, Bramante here gave the purest expression to his genius.

Table 6

Palazzo Farnese. Entrance. The monumentality of this grandiose 16th century palace is also evident in the simplicity and solemnity of the entrance portico.

Table 7

Palazzo Farnese. Exterior. This is the largest and most typical palace of the 16th century in Rome. It was erected for the family of Paul III during the period of their greatest prosperity. It was designed by Antonio da Sangallo the Younger and was completed by Michelangelo. After Sangallo's death in 1546, Michelangelo created the magnificent cornice above the façade and finished the upper story of the courtyard. He planned as well a connecting bridge to lead across the Tiber from the rear of the palace to the Villa Farnesina, but this grandiose idea was never realized.

Table 8

Palazzo Farnese. Windows on the ground floor. The architecture of the 16th century, even in the details of this princely palace, displays an extraordinary grandeur. Antonio da Sangallo, who planned this building, was also a great military architect.

Table 9

The "Facchino" Fountain. This is a typical 16th century fountain often deriving motifs from everyday life. This fountain shows an inn servant in the act of emptying a cask. It is to be found on the Corso. It is the work of an unknown sculptor of the middle of the century and is one of the so-called "speaking statues" (representing personages from popular satirical dialogues) the most famous of which is the "Pasquino."

Table 10–11

Ponte "rotto." This bridge, called the "Ponte rotto," is one of the many beautiful bridges of Rome, the most important being the Ponte Sisto and the Ponte Sant'Angelo. It dates from the 16th century. It was constructed by Nanni di Baccio Bigio in 1546, but it collapsed (as Michelangelo had predicted) in 1551. After being restored it collapsed a second time, in 1598, when the Tiber was in flood.

Table 12

Castel Sant'Angelo seen from the "Passetto." The Castel Sant'Angelo is to a great extent a structure dating from Roman Imperial times and was the Mausoleum of the Emperor Hadrian. In the Middle Ages and in the Renaissance it was transformed into a fortress and was thus the scene of dramatic events during the various sieges and uprisings. The "Passetto" (little passageway) is the characteristic long fortified corridor connecting the Vatican palaces with the Castel Sant'Angelo, constructed because the Popes and dignitaries wished to be able to reach the castle undisturbed during sieges.

Table 13

San Giovanni in Laterano. Façade of the transept. The simple and noble façade with the two-story loggia corresponds to the side of the basilica. It was constructed by Domenico Fontana in 1586. Behind it are to be seen the two symmetrical towers dating from the 14th century. The Egyptian obelisk is the most ancient and the largest of the obelisks in Rome, being 47 meters high. It was erected in Thebes fifteen centuries before Christ by Thutmes III. It was transported to Rome by Constans II and set up in the Circus Maximus. Sixtus V had it erected by Domenico Fontana in 1585 in the center of the new square.

Table 14

Caves of the Vatican. Monument to Paul II (detail). *Caritas.* The magnificent monument to the Venetian Pope Paul II, which is scattered in several parts, is the work of Mino da Fiesole and of his school. This delicate figure reveals the gentle manner of the Tuscan sculptor.

Table 15

Caves of the Vatican. Monument to Paul II (detail). Another figure by the school of Mino da Fiesole, probably the work of Giovanni Dalmata.

Table 16

Caves of the Vatican. Monument to Paul II (detail). One of the Angels belonging to the grandiose papal sepulchre.

Table 17

(cf. Table 14).

Table 18

Church of Santa Maria dell' Anima. Tomb of Hadrian VI (detail). The splendid monument erected to the Pope who was the teacher of Charles V is the work of various Tuscan artists (1523). Designed by Baldassare Peruzzi, the reclining statue of the Pope was carved by Niccolò Tribolo.

Table 19

Santa Maria del Popolo. Tomb of Girolamo Foscari. This is one of the most expressive mortuary figures of the 15th century in Rome. It was created by Lorenzo di Pietro, known as "il Vecchietto," of Siena. The figure of the defunct is impressive for the painterly handling of the folds and for the realism of the style.

Table 20–25

Caves of the Vatican. Monument to Sixtus IV (detail), the masterpiece of Antonio Pollaiolo. The great Tuscan sculptor and painter came to Rome in the time of Sixtus IV, after having completed various works, including the two bronze twins beneath the Etruscan she-wolf. In this great monument to Sixtus IV, the restorer of Rome and patron of artists, the sculptor shows in a new and original way the solemn presentation of the body of the Pontiff on a catafalque of gilt bronze as he had been exposed after his death, in St. Peters's. Around the figure of the Pope, commanding even in the sleep of death, are to be seen the Virtues also represented as lying in death, and on the elegant base are representations of the Arts and the Sciences, including the new science of Perspective, so important for the Renaissance. There are reproduced here: Music (Table 22) playing an organ bearing the emblem of Sixtus IV while an Angel works the bellows of the organ, Geometry (Table 23), Astrology (Table 24), Theology (Table 25) in the act of beholding the Light of the Truth.

Table 26

Detail of a frieze attributed to Jacopo Sansovino, of classical inspiration.

Table 27

Allegorical figure from one of the monuments of Andrea Sansovino in Santa Maria del Popolo.

Table 28–29

Church of Sant' Agostino. The "Madonna del Parto," by Jacopo Sansovino. Magnificent classical work carved under the influence of ancient statuary and the Moses of Michelangelo. It is one of the figures most venerated by the people of Rome. The imposing grandeur of the monumental group which suggests works of the Imperial Age has created among the ordinary people of Rome the legend to the effect that it is an ancient statue reworked by the artist.

Table 30

"Tortoise Fountain." The idea for this elegant and original fountain, one of the most beautiful of the Renaissance, was conceived by Giacomo della Porta, who designed the shells and the basin; the lively figures of the youths standing with one foot on a dolphin and pushing tortoises into the upper basin are the work of Taddeo Landini (1585), a skillful Florentine sculptor in bronze.

Table 31

Santa Maria del Popolo. Chigi Chapel. Statue of Jonah. This delicate and harmonious sculpture, inspired by classical art of the time of Hadrian (note the similarity with the face of Antony), was executed by the Florentine Lorenzetto, at the advice of Raphael, to whom tradition ascribes the conception of the statue.

Table 32

Vatican. Cappella Nicolina. Frescoes by Beato Angelico. In this detail the Pope is represented handing over the treasures of the church for distribution to the poor. This is a magnificent example of the spiritualized art of Angelico, who, after 1448, carried out for Nicholas V the pictorial decoration of this chapel built within a medieval tower. The frescoes relate the legends of Saints Stephen and Laurence, surrounded by the figures of other Saints. In some places the painter friar was assisted by Benozzo Gozzoli.

Table 33

Church of Santa Maria del Popolo. Assumption of the Virgin. By Tiberio d'Assisi, a pupil of Pinturicchio, who created various frescoes in Roman churches in the opening years of the 16th century. One of the best is the one shown here, its sweetness giving a good idea of the Umbrian manner.

Table 34

Galleria Borghese. Portrait of an unknown person, by Raphael. Around the year 1501, still under the influence of Perugino's manner and of the Flemish School, Raphael painted this beautiful and severe portrait which, according to different traditions, represents either Perugino or Pinturicchio.

Table 35

Galleria Borghese. The Lady with the unicorn, by Raphael (1505 or 1506). This suggestive portrait of a woman against a serene landscape seen through a loggia was identified by Roberto Longhi in 1927 as a work of Raphael. The painting was in the 17th century transformed into a St. Catherine by an unknown artist; in spite of the damage, the original was revealed in its purity in 1932, when the 17th century painting was removed.

Table 36–37

Villa Farnesina. The wedding of Alexander and Roxanna. By Sodoma. The two details representing the ladies attending upon the bride at her toilet (Table 36) and the face of Alexander the Great (Table 37) are part the decorative fresco executed by Sodoma for Agostino Chigi's bedchamber, in the Villa Farnesina (1511–1512).

Table 38–38

Villa Farnesina. Loggia of Psyche. These details are from a work by Raphael and pupils in the luxurious villa of Agostino Chigi (constructed by Baldassare Peruzzi in 1510–1511). They depict the myths of Psyche based on the stories of Apuleius. Raphael also painted in the loggia the famous "Galatea." The great artist shows us a large arbor and on the ceiling against the sky the Olympian deities in the clouds.

Table 40

St. Peter's. Pietà by Michelangelo (detail). This famous Pietà was executed for Cardinal Villier de la Groslaye and is a fine example of the new style of sculpture of the 16th century. The group was carved between 1499 and 1500 and is the only work signed by Michelangelo.

Table 41

Church of Santa Maria sopra Minerva. Christ Resurrected with the symbols of Redemption. Executed between 1514 and 1521 for Metello Vari and P. Castelloni, this Christ by Michelangelo is conceived as a heroic nude athlete displaying his trophies of victory.

Table 42–44

Church of San Pietro in Vincoli. Mausoleum of Julius II. The *Moses,* by Michelangelo. This extremely famous sculpture by Michelangelo was executed for the original large-scale design of the tomb of Julius II in St. Peter's: this was to have been one of forty-four statues disposed around the tomb of the Pope. Of these, in addition to the Moses, there remain the "Slaves"–in the Louvre and at the Academy in Florence, in part only sketched. After the long drawn out delay in the decision to proceed with the work–Michelangelo called it the "tragedy of the monument"–it was decided to utilize what had been completed in this mural tomb, in which Moses appears as the only statue which is entirely the work of Michelangelo.

Table 45

Sistine Chapel. Ceiling. The Prophet Jonah, by Michelangelo. Between 1508 and 1512 Michelangelo painted, at the order of Julius II, the entire ceiling of the Sistine Chapel with the story of Creation, the Prophets, sibyls and–in the lunettes–the forbears of Christ. The enormous fresco contains gigantic figures, like the Prophet Jonah in a new kind of perspective foreshortening.

Table 46–48

The Campidoglio. Michelangelo designed the over-all plan for three monumental buildings on the site of the medieval Castello, constructed on the ruins of the Tabularium and transformed in part into a palace: the Senatorial Palace in the center, the Palazzo dei Conservatori to the right and the Museum to the left, in a solemn and exalted architectural style, placing in the center of the square the statue of Marcus Aurelius (Table 48) dating from ancient Roman times, the sole remaining equestrian statue from Antiquity intact. The harmonious square on the "Sacred Hill" of Rome sums up the majestic and monumental character of the works in which the 16th century celebrated the dignity and the grandeur of the ancient world.

TEATRO

·OPVS
MINI

MVSIC

GEO
METRIA

ASTRO
LOGIA

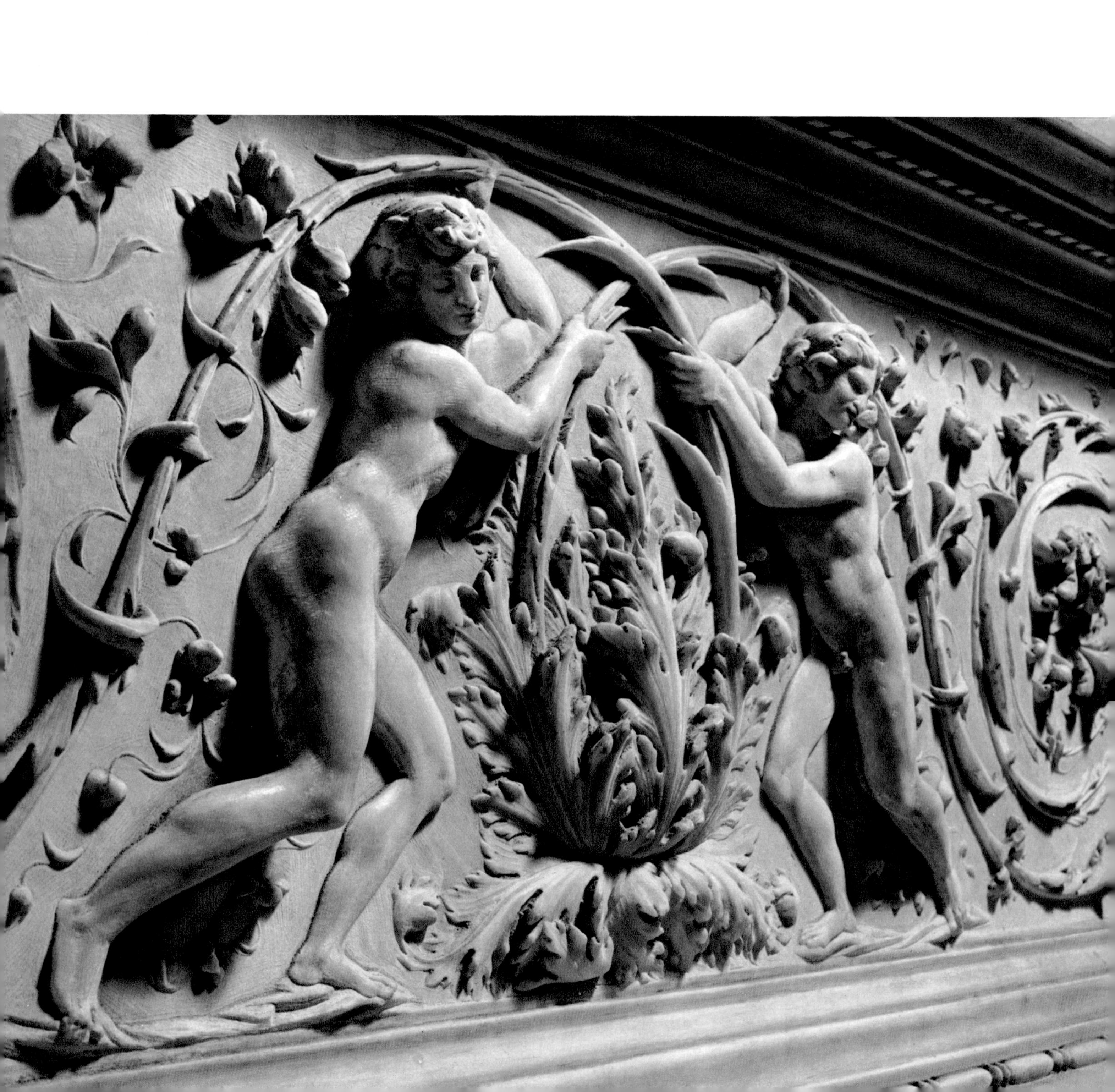

IONAS